孔子学院总部／
国家汉办汉语国际推广成都基地规划教材

走 进 天 府 系 列 教 材 【 成 都 印 象 】

悟道教

Exploring Daoism

西 南 财 经 大 学
汉语国际推广成都基地 著

西南财经大学出版社
中国·成都

西南财经大学
汉语国际推广成都基地 著

总策划 涂文涛

策 划
李永强

主 编
梁 婷 白巧燕

编 者
《成都印象·游成都》 胡倩琳
《成都印象·居成都》 郑 莹
《成都印象·吃川菜》 谢 娟 王 新
《成都印象·品川茶》 肖 静
《成都印象·饮川酒》 谢 娟
《成都印象·看川剧》 郑 莹
《成都印象·绣蜀绣》 谢 娟
《成都印象·梦三国之蜀国》 蒋林益 胡佩迦
《成都印象·悟道教》 沙莎 吕彦 陈茉
《成都印象·练武术》 邓 帆 刘 亚

审 订 冯卫东

英文翻译
Alexander Demmelhuber

Introduction

This textbook is one part of the "Into the Land of Plenty Teaching Series—Impressions of Chengdu".

This book's vocabulary follows the "Outline Vocabulary of the New HSK" and the lessons contained herein are designed accordingly. This book's main target group are foreign readers possessing a medium to high level of Chinese, making this book suitable for readers at the HSK 5 or 6 level. This textbook may not only be used in a structured classroom environment, but also in various teaching methods and self-study.This book introduces Daoist thinking and Daoist culture in the form of brief narrations and complementary dialogues. The characters in the book are adapted to the students of the Southwestern University of Finance and Economics. The selected stories are varied and practical, the language used is humorous and easy to understand in order to motivate students while also helping them understand Daoist culture and Daoist thinking.

This book is divided into six parts: what is Dao; Daoist philosophy and Daoist thinking; the difference between Daoist philosophy and Daoist religion; the influence of Daoist thinking and Daoist religion on Chinese culture; Daoist culture in Chengdu; and Daoist aphorisms. The book first presents the different interpretations of Daoism and then introduces the concepts of "naturalness" "tranquility""non-doing" etc. and their practical applications, followed by the differences between Daoist philosophy and Daoist religion. Readers then will be shown the tremendous influence and significance of Daoist thinking and Daoist religion on Chinese classical music, ancient Chinese paintings, health preservation and so on. Last is the introduction of famous Daoist places such as Mount Heming and Mount Qingcheng.

We, the authors, hope that the readers will be able to expand their horizons, getting to know Daoist thinking and Daoist culture and better understand the way Chinese act and behave, ultimately making our readers' lives in China even more varied and delightful.We hope that you will like Explore Daoism and we are looking forward to your opinions and suggestions. Hanban gave us much help and support during editing of this book and we would like to take this opportunity to express our gratitude.

前 言

此教材是《走进天府系列教材·成都印象》中的一本。

本书所使用词汇参照《新汉语水平考试词汇大纲》等级编排设计，主要面向具有中高级汉语水平的外国读者，适宜具有HSK5～6级水平的读者阅读。这本教材既适用于汉语教学机构的课堂教学，又可以满足各类教学形式和自学者的需求。

本书以简要叙述和补充对话相结合的形式向读者介绍了道家思想与道教文化，书中人物均以西南财经大学留学生为原型进行改编创作，所选故事情节丰富实用，语言幽默易懂，在调动学习者阅读兴趣的同时让其了解道教文化与道家思想。

本书分为"什么是'道'""道家与道家思想""道家和道教的区别""道家思想与道教对中国文化的影响""道教文化在成都"五个部分。书中首先介绍了对"道"的几种理解，介绍了道家"自然""清静""无为"等思想和在生活中的应用，对道家和道教加以区分，介绍了道家思想与道教对中国古典音乐、中国古代绘画、养生等方面的深远影响和意义，最后介绍了鹤鸣山、青城山等道教名山的一些情况。

编者希望读者阅读此教材后可以扩展视野，了解道家思想和道教文化，更好地理解中国人的部分处世哲学和行为习惯，在中国可以生活得更愉快、更充实。

希望您能喜欢我们的《悟道教》这本教材，也希望您对本书提出批评和建议。本书的编写得到了国家汉办的大力支持和帮助，在此一并表示感谢！

目录

第一课
[什么是 "道" ？]
Lesson 1　[What Is "Dao"?]

老子的《道德经》（又叫作《老子》），最初是一部哲学书，是道家哲学思想的重要来源，后来成为道教的经典。《道德经》分为"道经"和"德经"两部，合在一起称为《道德经》。

"道德"这个词跟现代汉语中的"道德"一词意思不同。当时，"道"与"德"并不是一个词，而是分开的，"道"生成宇宙万物，也是宇宙万物的规律，万物都应该遵守"道"，人们行动的时候也不例外。同时，"道"包含在宇宙万物之中，万物都体现出"道"的特点，这被称为"德"。老子认为，"道"是在宇宙产生之前就存在的，"道"是宇宙万物的来源，也是自然规律。

"道"在人们的生活中无处不在，影响着我们的生活、工作和养生。比如，一个人饿了要吃东西，累了想休息，渴了想喝水……这些就是很简单的"道"。如果一个人饿了不吃饭，累了不休息，那么就违反了这种自然规律，就是违反"道"；违反了"道"，身体就会出问题。当然，老子所说的"道"不仅仅是这么简单的问题，"道"涉及生活的方方面面。

再深一点的"道"就是：老子认为任何一种事物都会经历开始、发展、壮大这样几个阶段。就像人的一生会经历"出生、少年、壮年、老年、死亡"，花儿会经历"发芽、长叶子、开花"一样。所以，

① 高 峰　gāofēng
② 衰 落　shuāiluò
③ 凋 谢　diāoxiè
④ 顶 峰　dǐngfēng
⑤ 衰 老　shuāilǎo
⑥ 沮 丧　jǔsàng
⑦ 遵 循　zūnxún
⑧ 赌 注　dǔzhù
⑨ 冒 险　màoxiǎn
⑩ 评 估　pínggū

当一件事情发展到达顶峰的时候也就是它开始衰落的时候。就像人的生命顶峰是 30～50 岁，50 岁以后就开始慢慢地衰老了。就像花儿开得最美丽的时候，也就是花儿开始凋谢的时候。所以，一件事情发展到鼎盛的时候，我们不要太得意，说不定它就要开始衰落了；当我们刚刚开始工作的时候，感觉到艰难和吃力，也不要沮丧，万事开头难嘛。

比如说一个人刚刚开始学汉语，就想用复杂的词说复杂的句子，那么这就是不遵循"道"。而很多人刚开始学汉语觉得困难，也是很正常的，因为任何事物的开始都是有挑战的。再比如一个人刚刚到一个地方工作，这个人的能力可能只有 60 分，那么他做 55～65 分的事情就是遵循了"道"，如果他非要做 85 分或者 90 分的事情，就是违反了"道"，这就是一个赌注，可能会失败。所以，我们可以冒险，但是冒险之前一定要正确评估自己的能力。

Laozi's "Daodejing" (which can be translated as "The Book of the Way of Virtue"), also referred to as the "Laozi", was originally a philosophical book and the main origin of Daoist thinking. Later on, it became the fundamental text for religious Daoism. "Daodejing" has two parts, the "Daojing" and the "Dejing"; together they are called "Daodejing".

The meaning of "Daode" differs from its usage in modern Chinese. Back then, "dao" and "de" were not one single word; they were two words put together. "Dao" brought all things in the Universe into being and is also the law of all things in the Universe. All things have to abide by "dao", and people's actions are no exception. At the same time, "dao" implies that all things in the Universe express the characteristics of "dao", which is called "de". Laozi assumed that "dao" existed before the Universe came into being, that it is the source of all things in the Universe and that it is also the law of nature.

"Dao" is omnipresent in our daily lives and influences life, work and health. For example, if you are hungry, you want to eat; if you are tired, you want to rest; if you are thirsty, you want to drink, and so on. Simply put, these are all "dao". If you are hungry but do not eat, or tired but do not rest, then you violate this law of nature, which is "dao". If you violate "dao", your body will feel the consequences. Having said that, Laozi's usage of "dao" not only refers to such simple problems; "dao" is related to every aspect of life.

Let's go even deeper. Laozi assumes that everything goes through the same stages: "Beginning – Development – Expansion – Peak – Deterioration", which is just like our lives: "Birth – Youth – Prime – Agedness – Death" or those of flowers: "Sprout – Leaf out – Bloom – Wither". As we can see, once a thing reaches its peak, it starts to deteriorate. Just like with people, who reach their prime during ages 30, 40 and 50, they start to grow old once they are past their fifties. Just like flowers, which are most beautiful just when they begin to wither. So, once a thing reaches its state of splendidness, we should not get our hopes up, as it may start to deteriorate. Also, when we have just started to work and feel both challenged and exhausted, we should not lose hope, because we are at the beginning of our development stage, where the going is though.

Let's look at another example: If you just started to study Chinese and already want to use complicated words and phrases, then you do not abide by "dao". A lot of people think Chinese is difficult at the start, which is perfectly normal because every new beginning brings challenges. For instance, if you just arrived at a new place and started to work, you would probably only be able to perform 60% of work, so if you perform 55% or 65%, you abide by "dao". If you insist on performing 85% or 90%, you would violate "dao"; in this case, you are gambling and might be losing. We may take risks, but we have to accurately assess our abilities beforehand.

词语

高峰　沮丧

| 高峰 | gāofēng
peak, summit |
| 沮丧 | jǔsàng
depress; dispirit;dishearten |

shuāi luò 衰落	decline; deteriorate; go downhill
diāo xiè 凋谢	wither; wilt
dǐng fēng 顶峰	(fig.) high point
shuāi lǎo 衰老	age; grow old and weak

dǔ zhù 赌注	stake (in a gamble)
mào xiǎn 冒险	take risks; take chances
píng gū 评估	assess; evaluate
zūn xún 遵循	follow; abide by; comply with

专有名词

1. 老子　　　/ Lǎozǐ / Lao Tzu
2. 《老子》　/ Lǎozǐ / The Laozi
3. 《道德经》/ Dàodéjīng / Tao Te Ching

语法点

1.……，也就是……   2.非要

思考

> 这一课简单介绍了什么是"道"，你能结合生活和工作举一些与"道"相关的例子吗？

第二课　Lesson 2
〔道家与道家思想〕
〔Taoism Philosophy and Taoist Thinking〕

① 创始人　chuàngshǐrén
② 著作　zhùzuò
③ 顺其自然　shùnqí zìrán
④ 协调　xiétiáo
⑤ 遵循　zūnxún
⑥ 约束　yuēshù
⑦ 进取　jìnqǔ
⑧ 枯萎　kūwěi
⑨ 否则　fǒuzé
⑩ 违反　wéifǎn
⑪ 积聚　jī jù
⑫ 发挥　fāhuī
⑬ 适度　shìdù
⑭ 砍伐　kǎnfá
⑮ 除此之外　chúcǐ zhīwài
⑯ 派别　pàibié
⑰ 以静制动　yǐjìng zhìdòng
⑱ 以弱胜强　Yǐruò shèngqiáng
⑲ 以少胜多　yǐshǎo shèngduō
⑳ 以柔克刚　yǐróu kègāng
㉑ 天人合一　tiānrén héyī
㉒ 循序渐进　xúnxù jiànjìn
㉓ 深奥　shēn'ào

　　道家是中国古代的主要哲学派别之一，其创始人是中国古代春秋时期的老子，主要代表人物还有庄子等人，主要著作有《老子》（即《道德经》）、《庄子》等。

　　道家思想对中华哲学、文学、科技、艺术如音乐、养生、宗教等影响深远。请看几个重要的道家思想：

　　其一，自然。"自然"就是自然而然、顺其自然，让事物按照自身的特点自由发展，尊重自然，实现与自然的协调发展。作为个体来说，"自然"就是让我们保持自己的天性，做真正的自己，自在地生活。

　　其二，清静。"清静"是"清醒、冷静"的意思。遇事不要慌，要保持平和的心态。

　　其三，无为。"无为"不是什么都不做。"无为"的意思是不随意而为，不违"道"而为，不做无效的工作。对于符合"道"的事情，必须做，但是同时也要遵循自然规律。不争不抢，无身无欲。这种自我约束并非不求进取、消极被动的态度，而是向着一种更完满的目标，因而有着更积极的意义。

Daoist philosophy is one of ancient China's main schools of philosophy, whose founder was Laozi during China's Spring and Autumn period. Other notable representatives are, for example, Zhuangzi, and the main writings are "Laozi" (or "Daodejing"), "Zhuangzi" and so on.

Daoist thinking has greatly influenced Chinese philosophy, literature, science, technology, art, music, health, religion, and so on. Let's have a look at some important Daoist thoughts:

1.Naturalness. "Naturalness" means naturally of oneself; letting nature take its course; letting things freely develop according to their own traits; respecting nature; and develop together with nature in harmony. As for an individual, "naturalness" tells us to follow our nature, stay true to ourselves and live unrestrained.

2. Tranquility. Tranquility here means clear-headed and calm, not losing your head whatever happens, and keeping your coolness.

3. Non-action. "Non-action" does not mean doing nothing; it means not acting arbitrarily, not violating "dao" and not doing ineffective work. We must do work that is in accordance with "dao", but we also have to abide by the law of nature. Do not compete, do not rush to be the first and let go of yourself and your desires. This restriction of our egos is not about being complacent and adopting a passive attitude; it is about working towards a more fulfilling goal and has therefore a positive connotation.

江一华：

我还是不太懂这几个词的意思，你能举个例子吗？

大 萌：

你知道"拔苗助长"的故事吗？很久以前，有一个人为了让自己田地里的禾苗长得快，就把禾苗往上拔，结果禾苗反而枯萎了。这个故事告诉我们的道理就是要按照事物的发展规律做事，否则就会有不好的结果。

江一华：

我明白了，"自然"的意思就是不要违反自然规律，让事物自由发展。

文小西：

"清静"又是什么意思呢？我觉得热闹也很好啊！

大 萌：

"清静"的意思是说你做一件事的时候要保持内心的平静，不要太紧张，要清醒、冷静，如果你有很多情绪积聚在一起，你可能就做不好一件事。

江一华:

比如说，我们在学习的时候，如果一边玩手机一边学习，是不是效果就不太好了？如果要学习，就应该专心地学、安心地学，不要总想着玩儿，这是"清静"吗？

大 萌:

你说的也算是一种"清静"吧。

文小西:

还有考试以前如果太紧张了，总是害怕自己考不好，情绪不稳定，就没办法好好复习，考试的时候也很难发挥好，所以我们要保持"清静"的状态。那"无为"又是什么意思？就是什么都不做吗？

大 萌:

"无为"不是什么都不做，而是在遵循自然规律的前提下，不该做的不做，该做的必须做好；凡事都有一个度，超过那个度就会有不好的结果。比如说，我们学习汉语的时候，如果你每天学得太多了，就会记不住，虽然花费了很多时间和精力，但是效果并不好。所以我们既要"无为"，按照规律学习，又要"清静"，不能学得太多或者太少。

文小西：

　　你刚才说要"适度"，比如说经济发展和环境保护的问题，对热带雨林的过度砍伐虽然短期内会有一定的经济效益，但是从长远发展来看，会对人类社会和自然环境造成严重的破坏，"无为"就是要适度地开采，不能过度开采。

大　萌：

　　道家思想除此之外，还有"与时迁变""应物变化""物极必反""以静制动""以弱胜强""以少胜多""以柔克刚""天人合一"等很多思想。

江一华、文小西：

　　都是四个字的词啊！我最头疼的就是这些词了。

大　萌：

　　别着急，我们一步一步地学习。道家的思想可比我们说的要复杂和深奥多了。

Jiang Yihua: I still don't get the meaning of these words. Could you give an example?

Da Meng: Do you know the story of "Pulling Seedlings to Help Them Grow"? Once upon a time, somebody wanted to make the seedlings in the fields grow faster, so he pulled them upward and the seedlings consequently withered away. This story tells us that we should respect the development phases of all things, otherwise we will receive bad results.

Jiang Yihua: I got it. "Naturalness" means that we should not violate the law of nature and let all things develop freely.

Da Meng: Here is another example: if we are hungry, we want to eat; if we are tired, we want to rest; if we are thirsty, we want to drink. If you are hungry but do not eat, tired but do not rest, your body will feel the consequences. This is another expression of "naturalness".

Wen Xiaoxi: But what is "tranquility", again? Being lively is a good thing!

Da Meng: "Tranquility" means remaining level-headed whatever you do, being calm and sober rather than overly nervous. If a lot of emotions pile up together in you, you will probably do a bad job.

Jiang Yihua: If we, for example, are studying and are on our phones at the same time, the result would not be that great, right? If we want to study, we must focus on and keep our minds on studying rather than amusing ourselves. Is that what "tranquility" is all about?

Da Meng: You could say that, yes.

Wen Xiaoxi: Also, if we are too nervous before and during an exam because we are constantly afraid of getting a low score, we'll be emotionally unstable and won't be able to properly focus on studying; in the end, we will perform poorly during the exam. This is why we have to remain "tranquil". So, what about "non-action"? Is it about doing nothing at all?

Da Meng: "Non-action" is not about doing nothing at all. It is about abiding by the law of nature: don't do anything you aren't supposed to do, and do anything you should do; there is a limit to everything and once you're past that, the results won't be good. For example, if we study too much Chinese every day, we won't be able to remember it all. Although we spend a lot of time and energy, the result is anything but good. So we should take "non-action", meaning studying according to the law of nature, and also remain "tranquil", meaning we shouldn't study too much but also not too little.

Wen Xiaoxi: So we should do everything in moderation, right? Like when it comes to economic development and the protection of the environment, overly cutting down rainforests would result into certain profits in the short run, but, in the long run, would be detrimental to our societies and severely damage the environment. "Non-action" is about moderately, not excessively felling trees.

Da Meng: In addition to this, you may also find "change with the times, adapt to change", "things will turn into their opposite when they reach the extreme", "not be hasty in one's decisions" "use the weak to defeat the strong" "defeat the many with the few" "overcome hardness with softness" and "heaven and man are identical" as parts of Daoist thinking.

Jiang Yihua & Wen Xiaoxi: These are all words made up of four characters! Those give me the most trouble.

Da Meng: Don't worry, we'll study step by step. The lines of thought we find in Daoist philosophy are more complicated and profound than what we were just talking about.

词 语

约枭	砍伐
约束 yuēshù restrict; constraint	砍伐 kǎnfá fell (trees)

chuàng shǐ rén 创 始 人	founder; creator; initiator	jìn qǔ 进 取	keep forging ahead; eager to make progress
zhù zuò 著 作	work; book; writings	kū wěi 枯 萎	wilt; wither
shùn qí zì rán 顺 其 自 然	let nature take its course; take things as they come	fǒu zé 否 则	otherwise; if not; or else
xié tiáo 协 调	coordinate; concert;	wéi fǎn 违 反	violate (a law)
zūn xún 遵 循	follow; abide by; adhere to	jī jù 积 聚	accumulate; build up
bì shǔ 避 暑	avoid summer heat (by going to a cool place or a summer resort)		

fā huī 发 挥	bring into play; display; exhibit
chú cǐ zhī wài 除此之外	in addition to this

shì dù 适 度	moderately; appropriate
shēn ào 深 奥	profound

pài bié 派 别	school of thought; group; faction
yǐ jìng zhì dòng 以 静 制 动	be calm and reserved when reacting; not be hasty in one's decisions
yǐ ruò shèng qiáng 以 弱 胜 强	use the weak to defeat the strong
yǐ shǎo shèng duō 以 少 胜 多	defeat the many with the few
yǐ róu kè gāng 以 柔 克 刚	overcome hardness with softness
tiān rén hé yī 天 人 合 一	heaven and man are identical; man is an integral part of nature
xún xù jiàn jìn 循 序 渐 进	in sequence, step by step; make steady progress incrementally

专有名词

1. 道家　　/ Dàojiā / Daoist; follower of Dao

2. 庄子　　/ Zhuāngzǐ / Zhuangzi / Zhuang Zhou

3. 《庄子》 / Zhuāngzǐ / The Zhuangzi

语法点

1. 作为……来说　　2. 并非　　3. 既……又……

思考

1. 请结合自己的生活，谈谈你是怎么理解文章中提到的"自然""清静"和"无为"的。

2. 你是否同意文中的观点？为什么？

第三课 [道家和道教的区别]
Lesson 3 [The Difference Between Daoism as a Philosophy and as a Religion]

① 概 念　gàiniàn
② 派 别　pàibié
③ 先秦时期　Xiānqín shíqī
④ 形 成　xíngchéng
⑤ 创 始　chuàngshǐ
⑥ 教 主　jiàozhǔ
⑦ 经 典　jīngdiǎn
⑧ 摆 脱　bǎituō
⑨ 隐 居　yǐnjū
⑩ 土生土长　tǔshēng-tǔzhǎng
⑪ 仪 式　yíshì
⑫ 伦 理　lúnlǐ
⑬ 崇 拜　chóngbài
⑭ 继 承　jìchéng
⑮ 高 尚　gāoshàng
⑯ 有 毒　yǒudú
⑰ 欲 望　yùwàng
⑱ 综上所述　zōngshàng suǒshù

　　道家和道教是有区别的，不是同一个概念。

　　首先，道家是一个哲学派别，是先秦时期形成的。道家的创始人是老子，姓李，叫李耳，曾经当过管理图书的官员。他辞去工作后写了一本书叫《道德经》。老子后来被道教尊为教主，称为"太上老君"。《道德经》也成为道家和道教共同的重要经典。除了老子以外，道家最重要的代表人物还有庄子。道教是中国的本土宗教，是东汉时期形成的。道教的创始人是张道陵。张道陵年轻的时候读了很多书，很有学问。可是他觉得学到的知识都不能帮助他摆脱死亡，所以辞了官，去山里隐居，研究长生不老的办法。他到了四川以后，在鹤鸣山创立了教派，当时想加入他的教派的人都要交五斗米（即五十升米），所以他的教派被称作"五斗米道"。他以老子为教主，以《道德经》为主要经典，于是道教正式形成。后来张道陵又到了青城山，因为他被尊为"天师"，所以他在青城山住的地方叫作"天师洞"。

　　其次，道教作为中国土生土长的宗教，有独特的长生不老的信仰，有道教徒（道士）和道教组织，还有道教仪式和活动，而道家没有这些内容，道家追求的是精神上的自由。

最后，道教的思想来源比较复杂，除了道家思想以外，还有儒家的伦理思想、古代的鬼神崇拜、神仙信仰等。

（1）道家和道教的基本思想都是"道"，都把"道"看成宇宙的起源和规律。道教甚至认为老子也是"道"变成的，人如果能得"道"，就可以成为神仙，长生不老。

（2）儒家重视道德修养，道教也继承了儒家的这种观念，提出要成为神仙就必须有高尚的道德，要多做好事，不做坏事。

（3）古代的中国人相信"万物有灵"，太阳、月亮、河、山、植物等都有神灵在控制。他们也相信人死了以后会变成鬼。这些神鬼都能对活着的人做好事或者坏事。后来，这些神灵中有很多都成为道教的神。因此，道教是一种多神教。

（4）在中国，对神仙的信仰有很长的历史。传说中，神仙的样子跟人一样，可是能够长生不老。他们还有一些别的超能力，比如会飞，能治各种病，能让死去的人活过来，还可以随便改变自己的样子。如果一个普通人运气很好，碰见了神仙，而且从神仙那里得到神奇的药，那么这个普通人也可以成为神仙。从很早的时候开始，不少国王和皇帝就到处寻找神仙，吃"可以不死"的药，但是都没有成功。除了寻找神仙，道士们也开始试着自己做不死药，希望吃了以后变成神仙。可是，那些药都有毒，吃了以后死了不少人。后来道士就开始练习身体里的气和心。他们相信如果一个人能减少欲望，保持心情安静，再让气在身体里按一定的路线顺利地流动，就能健康长寿，甚至长生不老。

综上所述，道教和道家是不一样的，但是又有一定的联系。

Daoist philosophy and Daoist religion differ from each other. They are not the same concept.

First, Daoist philosophy is a school of philosophy that was formed before the foundation of the Qin Imperial Dynasty. Its founder was Laozi (an honorific title), whose personal given name was Li Er, with Li being his last name. He had been an official who managed books before he resigned and wrote a book called Daodejing. Laozi was later on worshipped as the founder of Daoist religion under the name "Supreme Old Lord". Daodejing is a fundamental text for both philosophical and religious Daoism. Apart from Laozi, Zhuangzi was another important representative of Daoist religion. Daoist religion is of Chinese origin and was formed during the Eastern Han Dynasty. Its founder was Zhang Daoling. He read a lot of books when he was young and was therefore very knowledgeable. However, he thought that all this knowledge did not help him to free himself from death, so he resigned from his office and went to the mountains to live in seclusion, where he studied methods of immortality. After his arrival in Sichuan, he founded a movement on Mount Heming. Those who wished to be part had to hand over five dou of rice (five pecks or fifty liters of rice), which is why his cult was called "Way of the Five Dou of Rice". Daoist religion was formerly founded when Zhang Daoling named Laozi as its founder and the Daodejing as its fundamental text. Later on, Zhang Daoling returned to Mount Qingcheng. Since he was referred to as "Celestial Master", the place where he lived on Mount Chingcheng was called "Grotto of the Celestial Master".

Second, Daoist religion is an indigenous religion in China and includes unique beliefs about immortality. It has followers, priests and organizations as well as rituals and activities. Daoist philosophy, on the other hand, lacks all of these; its practitioners only pursue spiritual freedom.

Third, the origins of Daoist religion are relatively complicated. Other than Daoist thinking, there are also Confucianism, ancient China's worship of spirits, the belief in Xian and so on, which play a part.

1. Daoist philosophy and Daoist religion are fundamentally founded on the "dao" and regard it as the origin and law of the Universe. In Daoist religion, it is even assumed that Laozi became the "dao"; if people are able to obtain the "dao", they can turn into Xian, immortal beings.

2. Confucianism attaches great importance to moral cultivation, which is a concept that religious Daoism carries on. It states that only a person of high morals may become a Xian, which can be done by doing good deeds and not bad deeds.

3. In ancient times, Chinese believed that all things had a spiritual essence, and that the sun, the moon, rivers and mountains, plants and so on all had a spirit that controls them. They also believed that people turned into spirits after death. These spirits can do good or bad things to people. Later, many of these spirits became deities of Daoist religion. Therefore, Daoist is a religion of polytheism.

4. The belief in Xian has had a long history in China. According to legends, the appearance of Xian is the same as of people, but they are immortal. They also possess other supernatural abilities, such as flying, curing any diseases, reviving the dead and changing their appearance at a whim. If an ordinary person is fortunate, he will come across a Xian and receive some mystical medicine, through which this person can also become a Xian. From very early on, kings and emperors went everywhere in the search of Xian and to have some of this immortality-bestowing medicine, but they all failed. Other than looking for Xian, Daoists began to try making their own immortality medicine in the hopes of turning into a Xian. However, this medicine turned out to be poisonous and killed a lot of people. Afterwards, Daoists started to train their life force and their minds. They believed if a person can reduce their desires, remain calm and let their life force within their bodies smoothly circulate along a certain path, they would live a long and health life and even become immortal.

To sum up, Daoist religion and Daoist philosophy are not the same, but they do share a certain connection.

文小西：

这几天真热！开着空调坐在家里都要流汗。

马 兰：

是啊，每天气温都是三十五六摄氏度。哎，你们那儿的夏天是怎么过的呢？

江一华：

我们家乡的人啊，夏天常常去旅游，孩子们参加夏令营什么的。最热的时候我们喜欢去凉快的地方或者海边避暑。

马 兰：

说到避暑，不如我们去青城山住两天吧，听说山上比这儿凉快多了。而且也不远，坐火车一个小时就到了。

大 萌：

好啊，择日不如撞日，我们收拾一下，过一会儿就出发吧。

（在火车上）

文小西：

青城山为什么叫青城山呢？我知道"青"是"绿"的意思，因为山上有很多树。"城"是什么意思呢？跟"城市"有关系吗？

大 萌：

　　"城"不是"城市"的意思。你知道"长城"的意思吗？

文 小西：

　　知道，是"great wall"。

大 萌：

　　"青城"的"城"和"长城"的"城"是一个意思，都是wall。"城"在古时候指"城墙"，所以"青城"是"green wall"。

马 兰：

　　哦，我还以为"青城"是绿色的城市呢。我听说青城山之所以很有名，是因为它是道教的发源地。

大 萌：

　　道教的发源地是鹤鸣山，在道教产生的过程中，青城山的地位也很重要。

文 小西：

　　那道教是在鹤鸣山创立的吗？是谁创立的？是不是老子？

大 萌：

道教是在鹤鸣山创立的，不过创始人不是老子，是张道陵。

江一华：

张道陵？没听说过这个人呢。

大 萌：

张道陵是汉代的人，离现在差不多有 2 000 年了。他年轻的时候是个儒生，读了很多书，很有学问。后来他觉得自己虽然知道很多东西，可是终有一天是要死的，他学的东西都不能帮助他摆脱死亡，所以辞了官，去山里隐居，研究长生的办法。

马 兰：

那他找到长生的办法了吗？

大 萌：

传说他找到了。找到长生的办法以后，他到了四川，在鹤鸣山创立了"五斗米道"，这是最早的道教派别。

文小西：

"五斗米道"这个名字好奇怪啊。

大 萌:

知道意思就不觉得奇怪了。"一斗"是"十升"，"五斗米"就是五十升米。因为想加入张道陵的教派的人都要交五斗米，所以叫作"五斗米道"。

江 一华:

就好像想要当孔子学生的人都要交一些肉一样，对吗？

大 萌:

对，就是那样的……马上要到了，我们准备下车吧。

江 一华、文小西、马兰:

好的。

We Xiaoxi: It's been so hot lately! Even with the AC on at home I'm still sweating.

Ma Lan: Yeah, every day it has 35 to 36 degrees (Celsius). Geez! How do you guys back at home pass the summer?

Jiang Yihua: People from my town often go travelling in the summer and the kids go summer-camping or whatever. On the hottest days we like going to cooler places or to the sea to avoid the heat.

Ma Lan: Talking about avoiding the heat, what about going to Mount Qingcheng for a few days? I heard that it's much cooler in the mountains. They're also not that far away; we can reach them in just one hour by train.

Da Meng: All right! No time like the present, get your stuff and we'll head out.

(Scene: on the train)

Wen Xiaoxi: Why is Mount Qingcheng called Qingcheng? I know that "qing" means "green" because there are a lot of trees in the mountains. What about "cheng", though? Is it associated with "town"?

Da Meng: "Cheng" does not mean "town". Do you know what "chang cheng" stands for?

Wen Xiaoxi: Sure, that's the Great Wall.

Da Meng: The "cheng" in "qing cheng" is the same as "cheng" in "chang cheng", they both mean "wall". "Cheng" in ancient times refers to "cheng qiang", so "qing cheng" means "green wall".

Ma Lan: Oh, and I thought "qing cheng" refers to a green town. I heard that the reason why Mount Qingcheng is so famous is that it is the birthplace of Daoist Religion.

Da Meng: That would be Mount Heming, but when religious Daoism came into being, Mount Qingcheng also became a place of importance.

Wen Xiaoxi: So religious Daoism was founded on Mount Heming? By whom? Was it Laozi?

Da Meng: Religious Daoism was indeed founded on Mount Heming, but its founder was not Laozi, but Zhang Daoling.

Jiang Yihua: Zhang Daoling? Never heard of him before.

Da Meng: Zhang Daoling lived during the Han Dynasty, which was 2,000 years ago. He was a Confucian student when he was young. He read a lot of books and was very knowledgeable. Later on, he thought that, although he knew so much, he still had to die one day, and everything that he learnt would not help him free from death. So he resigned from office, went to the mountains to live in seclusion and studied how to live forever.

Ma Lan: So did he succeed?

Da Meng: He did. After he found a way to live forever, he went to Sichuan and founded the "Way of the Five Dou of Rice" on Mount Heming, which was the earliest movement of religious Daoism.

Wen Xiaoxi: "Way of the Five Dou of Rice" sounds really strange.

Da Meng: If you know what the name stands for, you won't find it strange. "One dou" (one peck) is "ten liters", so "five dou of rice" are fifty liters of rice. Since everybody who wanted to enter Zhang Daoling's movement had to hand over five dou of rice, his movement was called "Way of the Five Dou of Rice".

Jiang Yihua: So it was like when those who wanted to study under Confucius had to hand over some meat, right?

Da Meng: Exactly… We're almost there, get ready to get off.

Jiang Yihua, Wen Xiaoxi & Ma Lan: All right.

词 语

士生士长 | 隐居

士 生 土 长	tǔshēng-tǔzhǎng locally born and bred; indigenous; home-grown

隐 居	yǐnjū live in seclusion; with draw from society

gài niàn 概 念	concept; idea
pài bié 派 别	school of thought; group; faction
Xiān Qín shí qī 先 秦 时 期	pre-Qin days (before 221 BC when the First Emperor of Qin united China)
xíng chéng 形 成	form; become; take shape
chuàng shǐ 创 始	initiate; found

jiào zhǔ 教 主	founder or leader of a religion or sect; revered figure
jīng diǎn 经 典	scriptures
bǎi tuō 摆 脱	break away from; get rid of; free oneself from
yí shì 仪 式	ceremony; rite; ritual
lún lǐ 伦 理	ethics

chóng bài 崇拜	worship
gāo shàng 高尚	noble; lofty
yù wàng 欲望	desire

jì chéng 继承	inherit; carry on
yǒu dú 有毒	poisonous; toxic
zōng shàng suǒ shù 综上所述	to summarize; in summary

专有名词

1. 东汉 / Dōnghàn / Eastern Han Dynasty (公元 25-220 年)

2. 鹤鸣山 / Hèmíng Shān / Mount Heming

3. 青城山 / Qīngchéngshān / Mount Qingcheng

4. 太上老君 / Tàishàng Lǎojūn / Supreme Old Lord

5. 张道陵 / Zhāng Dàolíng / Zhang Daoling

6. 先秦 / Xiānqín / Pre-Qin days (i.e. before 221 BC when the First Emperor of Qin united China)

语 法 点

1. 以……为……   2. 之所以

思 考

1. 用自己的话简单说说道家和道教的区别有哪些。

2. 道教的思想来源有哪些？

三生万物。上善若水。自然之道静，故天地万物生。道以清净为本。

树克天于不知足。道可道，非常道。道生一，一生二，二生三。

人法地，地法天，天法道，道法自然。

天道无为，任物自然。

养生之方，唯不及远。行不疾步，耳不极听，目不久视，坐不至久，卧不及疲。

第四课
Lesson 4
[道家思想与道教对中国文化的影响]
[The Influence of Daoist Thinking and Daoist Religion on Chinese Culture]

文小西：

道家的主要思想以及道教对中国人和中国文化有什么影响呢？

大萌：

影响太多了，不过我先听听你们的想法。

江一华：

我认为对人们的思想有影响，比如说道家思想里有"自然""清静"和"无为"。我学习了这些思想后，做事情就知道要顺其自然，遇到困难，也知道保持清醒和冷静，遇到问题好好想解决的办法，如果不能解决，也不会那么自责或者遗憾，学会了保持平和的心态。

大萌：

说得有道理！

① 演 奏　　yǎnzòu
② 乐 器　　yuèqì
③ 娴 熟　　xiánshú
④ 精 神　　jīngshén
⑤ 气 质　　qìzhì
⑥ 神 韵　　shényùn
⑦ 境 界　　jìngjiè
⑧ 形神俱妙　xíngshén jùmiào
⑨ 讲 究　　jiǎngjiu
⑩ 形 似　　xíngsì
⑪ 神 似　　shénsì
⑫ 意 境　　yìjìng
⑬ 回味无穷　huíwèi wúqióng
⑭ 疲 劳　　píláo
⑮ 禁 忌　　jìnjì
⑯ 避 免　　bìmiǎn
⑰ 贪 心　　tānxīn
⑱ 以 致　　yǐzhì
⑲ 养 生　　yǎngshēng
⑳ 理 念　　lǐniàn
㉑ 调 理　　tiáolǐ
㉒ 知 足　　zhīzú
㉓ 隐 含　　yǐnhán
㉔ 自 责　　zìzé
㉕ 超 脱　　chāotuō
㉖ 良药苦口　liángyào kǔkǒu

文小西：

> 我学过中国画，中国画讲究的是"神似"而不是"形似"，画者运用绘画技巧，把自己的想法与笔墨或者颜料相结合，画出心中所想，表达自己的追求和理念，讲究"意境深远""回味无穷"。这都跟道家和道教中自然、超脱的思想有关系。

江一华：

> 在音乐方面也是。演奏乐器时，演奏者不仅要有娴熟的技巧，还要把自己内在的精神气质和乐曲结合起来，演奏出"神韵"，这是乐器演奏者追求的最高境界，即"形神俱妙"。绘画、书法、戏剧、舞蹈等其他形式也是如此。

大萌：

> 说完了艺术，我们再来说说"养生"。

文小西：

> 养什么？我知道养花、养草、养猫，"生"是什么？

大萌：

> "生"就是"生命"。"养生"就是让你的身体健康。

江一华：

> 每天晚上在公园里有很多老人跳舞，这也是一种养生的方式吗？

大 萌：

对，这是有中国特色的养生方式，你们也可以试一试。

江 一华：

哈哈哈，那我们一定很受欢迎。

文 小西：

那道家的养生指的是什么呢？

大 萌：

道家养生讲究"静""少""动""忌"。"静"是清静无为，控制欲望。"少"是少思考、少焦虑。"动"的意思是运动养生，不要疲劳。"忌"则是养生的禁忌，即养生中要避免的情况，比如不能太饿了才吃饭、太渴了才喝水，吃饭的时候不要吃得太快太饱，喝水时不要喝得太多太急，要适度。道家的养生有心理养生、生理养生等。也就是说，道家的养生理念不仅让人身体健康，也关注人的思想健康。

大 萌：

比如《道德经》的《养生篇》中就有"祸莫大于不知足"这样的句子，意思是不知道满足是最大的祸患，以致造成心理上的不健康。

文小西：

大萌，道家和道教对中医药也有影响，对吗？

大 萌：

对，道教对中医学和中药学都有非常深远的影响。学校的中医药讲座你们去听了吗？

江一华：

我去听了。现在我也常去按摩，身体不舒服的时候也会去吃点中药什么的，不过有的中药实在太苦啦。

大 萌：

良药苦口嘛。道教文化里有一个主要的内容——"长生不老"和"长生不死"。所以古代的道士就研究出了很多他们认为可以长生不老和不死的药，要研究吃什么对身体好，通过养生达到长生不老、长生不死的目的。中医也吸收了道教文化中一些好的养生方法，所以有句俗话是"十道九医"，就是说十个道士里大概有九个都懂一点医学知识。

Wen Xiaoxi: What kind of influence do the main ideology of Daoist philosophy and Daoist religion have on Chinese culture?

Da Meng: A huge one. But I'd like to hear your ideas first.

Jiang Yihua: I think that they influence the way people think. For example, "naturalness" "tranquility" and "non-action" are part of Daoist philosophy, and after having studied them, I now know that I have to let nature take its course whatever I do; whenever I find myself in a tough spot, I know now that I have to remain calm and sober; whenever I run into problems, I have to carefully consider how to solve those, and if I don't succeed, I shouldn't overly blame myself or have regrets, instead I learn how to keep my cool.

Da Meng: Sounds very reasonable!

Wen Xiaoxi: I studied traditional Chinese painting, which emphasizes "similarity in spirit" rather than "similarity in shape". Painters use painting techniques to link their thoughts with ink or pigments, and thus paint their thoughts from deep within, giving expression to their own aspirations and beliefs. Throughout this process, they emphasize "profound artistic conception" and want to leave a lasting impression on those who gaze upon their paintings. This style of painting is closely linked with naturalness and transcending thinking as they can be found in philosophical and religious Daoism.

Jiang Yihua: The same applies to music. When playing an instrument, the performer must not only be skilled in their techniques, they also have to link their inner ethos with the music to charm their audience – this is every performer's highest aspiration: unity of form and spirit, the ability to not only achieve technical prowess, but also to resonate with the audience. This applies to painting, calligraphy, theater, dance and so on.

Da Meng: Now that we've finished talking about the arts, let's talk about "yang sheng" (preserve one's health).

Wen Xiaoxi: What does "yang" mean here? I know it's used for flowers, grass and cats, where it means "raise, keep or grow". What does "sheng" mean?

Da Meng: "Sheng", as in "sheng ming", means life. "Yang sheng" means keeping your body healthy.

Jiang Yihua: Every night in the park there are lots of elderly people dancing; is that also a form of maintaining your health?

Da Meng: It is. It is also very Chinese way of health preservation. You should give it a try!

Jiang Yihua: Haha, we'd be pretty popular!

Wen Xiaoxi: So what about health maintenance in Daoist philosophy?

Da Meng: Daoist philosophy stresses "calmness" "less" "action" and "taboo". "Calmness" refers to tranquility and non-Action, the control of your desires. "Less" means less thinking, less pondering. "Action" means exercising and maintaining your health, not giving into fatigue. "Taboo" refers to the taboos of maintaining your health that you need to avoid: for example, you shouldn't be too hungry before eating and not too thirsty before drinking; while eating, don't eat too fast or too much, while drinking, don't drink to much or too fast – keep everything in moderation. In Daoist philosophy, maintaining your health includes, but is not limited to maintaining your psychological and physical heath. In other words, Daoist practices of health maintenance are not only concerned about maintaining a healthy body, but also a healthy mind.

Da Meng: For example, there is a chapter about health maintenance in *Daodejing* that contains this sentence: "No calamity is greater than discontentment", which means that not knowing satisfaction is the biggest calamity of them all. In other words, greed twists people's minds and, consequently, leads to an unhealthy mind.

Wen Xiaoxi: Da Meng, Daoist philosophy and religion also influence traditional Chinese medicine, right?

Da Meng: Right. Religious Daoism has had a very profound influence on both traditional Chinese medicine and traditional Chinese pharmacology. Have you been to the lectures on traditional Chinese medicine at our school?

Jiang Yihua: I have. Now, I often get massages and have some Chinese medicine whenever I don't feel well, and so on. I have to say, though, Chinese medicine is way to bitter.

Da Meng: Well, good medicine tastes bitter. Another important focus of Daoist culture lies in "eternal youth" and "immortality". Therefore, during ancient times, followers of religious Daoism did research on medicine which they thought would make people live forever young and on food that is good for our health. They assumed that we can achieve eternal youth and immortality through health maintenance. Traditional Chinese medical science also assimilated some good health maintenance methods from Daoist culture. This is the reason why there is the saying, "Ten Daoists, Nine Doctors", which means that in a group of ten Daoists, there are about nine who have some medical knowledge.

词 语

疲 劳	píláo fatigue; tired; fatigued; weary

贪 心	tānxīn greed; avarice

yǎn zòu 演 奏	perform on a musical instrument
yuè qì 乐 器	musical instrument
xián shú 娴 熟	adept; skilled
jīng shén 精 神	spirit; mind; consciousness; thought; essence
qì zhì 气 质	temperament; disposition; qualities; makings; personality traits
shén yùn 神 韵	charm or grace (in poetry or art)

jìng jiè 境 界	boundary; level
xíng shén jù miào 形 神 俱 妙	have both form and spirit;be both technically perfect and alluring
jiǎng jiu 讲 究	stress; be particular about; pay attention to
xíng sì 形 似	similarity in form;alike in form
shén sì 神 似	similarity in spirit; alike in spirit
yì jìng 意 境	mood of a literary work or a work of art; artistic conception

huí wèi wú qióng 回 味 无 穷	thought-provoking; memorable; lingering in memory; lasting
jìn jì 禁 忌	taboo
bì miǎn 避 免	avoid; refrain from
yǐ zhì 以 致	(usually referring to bad results) consequently; as a result
lǐ niàn 理 念	belief; conviction
tiáo lǐ 调 理	nurse one's health; recuperate

zhī zú 知 足	content with one's situation; know contentment
yǐn hán 隐 含	imply
zì zé 自 责	blame oneself
chāo tuō 超 脱	stand aloof; be unconventional
liáng yào kǔ kǒu 良 药 苦 口	Good medicine tastes bitter.

专有名词

1. 中医学　/ Zhōngyīxué / Traditional Chinese Medicine
2. 中药学　/ Zhōngyàoxué / Traditional Chinese Pharmacology

语法点

1. 以致　　2. ……，即……　　3. 于

思考

1. 道家思想与道教对中国文化有哪些影响？请举例说明。
2. 道家的"养生"指的是什么？你对"养生"的看法是什么？

第五课
Lesson 5

[道教文化在成都]

[Daoist Culture in Chengdu]

大 萌：

四川是道教的重要发源地。成都市内的青羊宫以及附近的鹤鸣山、青城山便具有代表性，都是著名的道教圣地。青羊宫在成都市内，一环路西二段，被誉为"川西第一道观"，也是全国著名的道教宫观之一；始建于周朝，后来被毁，现存建筑大多为清代陆续重建的；占地约4 800平方米，有山门、三清殿、唐王殿等建筑，高大雄伟，环境优雅，道教建筑特色突出。

江一华：

我们去过青城山了。

大 萌：

那我先说鹤鸣山吧。鹤鸣山是中国道教的发源地，道教名山之一，位于成都西部大邑县西北处，距离成都市区大概80千米，海拔1000余米。那儿山势雄伟，林木繁茂，有众多名胜古迹，是著名的风景旅游区和避暑胜地。

① 发 源　　fāyuán
② 陆 续　　lùxù
③ 雄 伟　　xióngwěi
④ 繁 茂　　fánmào
⑤ 避 暑　　bìshǔ
⑥ 遗 产　　yíchǎn
⑦ 郁郁葱葱　yùyù cōngcōng
⑧ 遗 迹　　yíjì
⑨ 开 创　　kāichuàng
⑩ 肥 沃　　féiwò
⑪ 灌 溉　　guàngài
⑫ 繁 华　　fánhuá

江一华：

　　我来说说青城山。它是一座有千百年历史的活的道教"博物馆"，是世界文化遗产，中国四大道教名山之一，道教发源地之一。青城山位于都江堰市西南，距离成都市区68千米，海拔1 000余米。那儿鸟语花香，树林郁郁葱葱，风景非常漂亮，享有"青城天下幽"的美誉。青城山分为前山和后山。前山有很多道宫和道观，后山有神秘的洞、大蜀王遗迹。前山的人文景观要多一些；后山有一些人文景观，但是以自然风光为主。

大萌：

　　"拜水都江堰，问道青城山"。青城山附近还有都江堰水利工程景区，战国时期的李冰是开创人。都江堰水利工程建造于公元前256年，已经有两千多年的历史了。都江堰建成至今，成都从来没有发生过水灾和旱灾，成为土地肥沃、富裕繁华的"天府之国"。

Da Meng: Sichuan is an important place of origin of religious Daoism. Within Chengdu you will find Qingyang Palace and in the surrounding areas there are Mount Hemin and Mount Qingcheng. Qingyang Palace, which is located in West Section 2 of the First Ring Road, is also called "Sichuan's first Daoist temple" and is one of China's most famous Daoist temples. It was first built during the Zhou Dynasty and later on destroyed. Most of the existing buildings were one after another rebuilt during the Qing Dynasty. It covers an area of about 4,800 square meters and boasts buildings such as Sanmen Gate, Sanqing Hall, Tangwang Hall and so on. The temple is both tall and majestic; its surroundings are elegant. The buildings possess prominent features of Daoist architecture.

Jiang Yihua: We've been to Mount Qingcheng.

Da Meng: Then let's talk about Mount Hemin first. Mount Hemin is the birthplace of Daoism and one of the famous Daoist mountains. It is located in Dayi County, which is in the west of Chengdu, about 80 kilometers away from the urban area, and in the northwest of Sichuan, at an altitude of more than 1,000 meters. There are majestic mountains, lush forests and many historical sites and scenic spots. It is a famous scenic tourist area and summer resort.

Jiang Yihua: Mount Qingcheng next. It is a living Daoist "museum" with thousands of years of history, a world cultural heritage, one of the four famous Daoist mountains in China, and one of the birthplaces of religious Daoism. Mount Qingcheng is located in the southwest of Dujiangyan City, which is 68 kilometers away from Chengdu, at an altitude of more than 1,000 meters. Over there, you can enjoy birdsongs and fragrant flowers, green and luxuriant forests and the very beautiful scenery. It has a reputation of being one of the most serene places in China. Mount Qingcheng is divided into front and back mountains. The former has a lot of Daoist palaces and temples, while the latter has mysterious caves and the remains of the former king of Shu (now Sichuan). The front mountains have a lot of places of cultural interest, while the back mountains also have those, but primarily boast natural sceneries.

Wen Xiaoxi: There's a saying that goes like this, "Go to Dujiangyan to appreciate the water and to Mount Qingcheng to worship Daoism". Near Mount Qingcheng is the Dujiangyan Irrigation System and Scenic Area, which was pioneered by Li Bing during the Qin Dynasty. The Dujiangyan irrigation system was built in 256 BC and has a long history of more than two thousand years. Since the completion of Dujiangyan, Chengdu has never gone through floods and droughts, turning into a flourishing "land of plenty" with fertile land.

词 语

避暑

避暑 bìshǔ
avoid summer heat (by going to a cool place or a summer resort)

繁茂

繁茂 fánmào
(of vegetation) lush and flourishing

fā yuán 发 源	rise; originate; source
lù xù 陆 续	one after another; in succession
xióng wěi 雄 伟	grand; imposing; magnificent; majestic
féi wò 肥 沃	(of soil) fertile; rich
yù yù cōng cōng 郁 郁 葱 葱	lush and green; green and luxuriant; verdant and lush

guàn gài 灌 溉	irrigate; water
fán huá 繁 华	flourishing; prosperous; bustling
yí chǎn 遗 产	heritage; legacy
kāi chuàng 开 创	initiate; start; found; pioneer; set up
yí jì 遗 迹	historical remains; remnant

专有名词

1. 青羊宫 / Qīngyáng Gōng / Qingyang Palace
2. 李冰 / Lǐ Bīng / Li Bing
3. 成都平原 / Chéngdū Píngyuán / the Chengdu Plain
4. 都江堰水利工程 / Dūjiāngyàn Shuǐlìgōngchéng / the Dujiangyan Irrigation System

语法点

1. 被……为…… 　　2. 之一

思考

1. 你去过哪些道教的道场？有什么特色？
2. 请简单介绍一下"都江堰水利工程"。

附 录

[Appendix]

道家格言

1. 人法地，地法天，天法道，道法自然。

2. 祸莫大于不知足。

3. 道可道，非常道。

4. 道生一，一生二，二生三，三生万物。

5. 上善若水。

6. 自然之道静，故天地万物生。

7. 道以清静为本。

8. 天道无为，任物自然。

9. 养生之方，唾不及远，行不疾步，耳不极听，
   目不久视，坐不至久，卧不及疲。

10. 养生者以不损为本，进道者以无病为先。

11. 万物之中，人最为贵。

12. 道大，天大，地大，人亦大。

13. 以道观之，物无贵贱。

14. 形神俱妙，与道合真。

Daoist Aphorisms

1.Man follows the earth, the earth follows the heaven, the heaven follows dao and dao follows naturalness.

2. No calamity is greater than discontentment.

3. The Dao that can be described is not the eternal Dao.

4. The Dao bears sensation, sensation bears memory, sensation and memory bear abstraction, and abstraction bears all the world.

5. Water benefits everything.

6. The method of naturalness proceeds in tranquility, and so it was that heaven, earth, and all things were produced.

7. The Dao is tranquility.

8. The Way of Heaven is non-action, and all things are naturalness.

9. How to maintain your health: Do not sleep too much; do not walk so much that your feet hurt; do not hear so much that your ears hurt; do not overuse your eyes; do not sit too long; do not go to bed unless you are tired.

10. Practitioners of health maintenance should avoid harm to themselves and Daoists should primarily avoid falling ill.

11. Of all things, man is the most precious.

12.The Dao is big, the Heaven is big, the Earth is big, and the man is big.

13.In terms of Taoism, things are neither cheap nor precious.

14.The body and the spirit are wonderful and true.

图书在版编目（CIP）数据

成都印象／西南财经大学 汉语国际推广成都基地著 —成都：西南财经
大学出版社，2019.7
（走进天府系列教材）
ISBN 987-7-5504-3776-0

Ⅰ．①成… Ⅱ．①西… Ⅲ．①汉语—对外汉语教学—教材②成都—
概况 Ⅳ．①H 195.4②K 927.11
中国版本图书馆 CIP 数据核字（2018）第 241717 号

走进天府系列教材：成都印象·悟道教
ZOUJIN TIANFU XILIE JIAOCAI:CHENGDU YINXIANG · WU DAOJIAO

西南财经大学 汉语国际推广成都基地 著

策 划：王正好 何春梅
责任编辑：李 才
装帧设计：张艳洁
插 画：辣点设计
责任印制：朱曼丽

出版发行	西南财经大学出版社（四川省成都市光华村街 55 号）
网 址	http：//www.bookcj.com
电子邮件	bookcj@ foxmail.com
邮政编码	610074
电 话	028-87353785
照 排	上海辣点广告设计咨询有限公司
印 刷	四川新财印务有限公司
成品尺寸	170mm×240mm
印 张	46.5
字 数	875 千字
版 次	2019 年 7 月第 1 版
印 次	2019 年 7 月第 1 次印刷
印 数	1-2050 套
书 号	ISBN 978-7-5504-3776-0
定 价	198.00 元（套）